The Yi King Or Book Of Changes:

The Oldest Work Of Magic 1143

B.C.

Charles F. Horne

Kessinger Publishing's Rare Reprints

Thousands of Scarce and Hard-to-Find Books
on These and other Subjects!

- Americana
- Ancient Mysteries
- Animals
- Anthropology
- Architecture
- Arts
- Astrology
- Bibliographies
- Biographies & Memoirs
- Body, Mind & Spirit
- Business & Investing
- Children & Young Adult
- Collectibles
- Comparative Religions
- Crafts & Hobbies
- Earth Sciences
- Education
- Ephemera
- Fiction
- Folklore
- Geography
- Health & Diet
- History
- Hobbies & Leisure
- Humor
- Illustrated Books
- Language & Culture
- Law
- Life Sciences

- Literature
- Medicine & Pharmacy
- Metaphysical
- Music
- Mystery & Crime
- Mythology
- Natural History
- Outdoor & Nature
- Philosophy
- Poetry
- Political Science
- Science
- Psychiatry & Psychology
- Reference
- Religion & Spiritualism
- Rhetoric
- Sacred Books
- Science Fiction
- Science & Technology
- Self-Help
- Social Sciences
- Symbolism
- Theatre & Drama
- Theology
- Travel & Explorations
- War & Military
- Women
- Yoga
- *Plus Much More!*

We kindly invite you to view our catalog list at:
http://www.kessinger.net

THE YI KING

OR

BOOK OF CHANGES

" *By fifty years' study of the Yi, I might come to be free from serious error.*"

— CONFUCIUS.

" *As I came not into life with any knowledge of it, and as my likings are for what is old, I busy myself in seeking knowledge there.*"

— CONFUCIUS.

THE YI KING

(INTRODUCTION)

LEARNED Chinamen even of our own day will sometimes assert that all our Western scientific knowledge,
our study of electricity, heat, light, and so on, is all con-
tained in the Yi King. They tell us that the eight "trigrams" at the basis of the Yi symbolize all this knowledge,
and that it was all known to their ancient magicians. They
admit, however, that they themselves had lost the power to
read these mighty truths from the pages of the Yi; and
Westerners are not likely to take too seriously its forgotten
mysteries.

The Yi King, as explained in our introduction, consists
of a series of diagrams of unknown but very vast antiquity,
and of the much more modern commentaries upon these.
The diagrams are now sixty-four in number, but may have
been originally only eight. These eight are made up by
taking two lines, one continuous and the other broken in the
middle, and setting them one above the other to form three
lines or trigrams, varying the relative order of the two
species of line in every possible manner. A glance at the
accompanying cut of the diagrams will make this clear, as
also how from the eight possible trigrams, sixty-four hexagrams or combinations of six lines have been made by unit-
ing each trigram with itself and with each other trigram.
To the original trigrams very ancient mystical meanings
were attached, one typifying the heavens, another high
mountains, and so on, as shown in the cut. Each also
represented a point of the compass.

These trigrams and hexagrams are the most ancient
known instrument of magic. They are still employed for
"casting lots"; and decisions for important occasions are
reached by appeal to them. This is done by reading the

FU-HSI'S TRIGRAMS

1	2	3	4	5	6	7	8
chien	tui	li	chan	sun	khan	kan	khwan
Heaven, the sky.	Water, collected as in a marsh or lake.	Fire, as in lightning; the sun.	Thunder.	The wind; wood.	Water, as in rain, clouds, springs, streams, and defiles. The moon.	Hills, or mountains.	The earth.
S.	S.E.	E.	N.E.	S.W.	W.	N.W.	N.
Untiring strength; power.	Pleasure; complacent satisfaction.	Brightness; elegance.	Moving, exciting power.	Flexibility; penetration.	Peril; difficulty.	Resting; the act of arresting.	Capaciousness; submission.

marks on tortoise-shells or the arrangement of the stalks of the "Chi" plant, such as still grows by the grave of Confucius. These markings direct the soothsayer to one and another of the diagrams, and by the significance of these he judges of the future.

Something more than magic was brought into the Yi when in 1143 B.C. the celebrated Duke Wan (afterward known as King Wan, founder of the Chau Dynasty) was cast into prison by a tyrant king. Wan wrote in his cell an interpretation of the sixty-four hexagrams, or rather a moral preachment based upon them. Soon afterward Wan's son, the Duke of Chau, added his commentary to that of his father. These constitute the present text of the Yi. The sixty-four commentaries are divided into two very similar sections, of which only the first is given in this volume. It discusses the first thirty, and perhaps more sacred, hexagrams.

To this text of the Yi, later writers have added ten appendixes which are now accepted as being almost equally sacred with the older Yi. Most of them are attributed to Confucius himself; but Western scholars are loth to credit this, partly because there is textual evidence against it, partly because the thought of the appendixes is generally so far below the usual high level of the Master's work. The Appendix which has been most admired is the fifth, which is here selected for reproduction.

There can be no question that Confucius was greatly interested in the Yi. We are told that he gave two years to a study of its first two diagrams, and that he said in his old age, "If I could be assured of sufficient more years to my life I would give fifty of them to the study of the Yi. Then I should be master of it." This attitude is characteristic of the sage, both in his reverence for the wisdom of the past and his confidence in the power of the human will, a confidence far removed from personal vanity. "Give me," said Archimedes, "a place to rest my lever, and I can move the earth." "Give me," implied Confucius, "sufficient time to think it all out, and I can understand the universe." Both philosophers were wrong. Their efforts would have been thwarted by larger difficulties than they could even imagine. Yet the remarks stand side by side as exemplars of the height to which man's faith and courage can rise. And of the two ideas that of Confucius is the more sublime.

THE YI KING

SECTION I

I. The Chien Hexagram

Explanation of the entire figure by King Wan.[1]

Chien represents what is great and originating, penetrating, advantageous, correct and firm.

Explanation of the separate lines by the Duke of Chau.

1. In the first or lowest line, undivided, we see its subject as the dragon lying hid in the deep. It is not the time for active doing.

[1] The text under each hexagram consists of one paragraph by King Wan, explaining the figure as a whole, and of six (in the case of hexagrams 1 and 2, of seven) paragraphs by the Duke of Chau, explaining the individual lines. The explanatory notices to this effect will not be repeated.

Each hexagram consists of two of the trigrams of Fu-hsi, the lower being called "the inner," and the one above "the outer." The lines, however, are numbered from one to six, commencing with the lowest. To denote the number of it and of the sixth line, the terms for "commencing" and "topmost" are used. The intermediate lines are simply "second," "third," etc. As the lines must be either whole or divided, technically called strong and weak, *yang* and *yin*, this distinction is indicated by the application to them of the numbers "nine" and "six." All whole lines are "nine," all divided lines, "six."

Does King Wan ascribe four attributes here to Chien, or only two? According to Appendix IV, always by Chinese writers assigned to Confucius, he assigns four, corresponding to the principles of benevolence, righteousness, propriety, and knowledge in man's nature. Chu Hsi held that he assigned only two, and that we should translate, "greatly penetrating," and "requires to be correct and firm," two responses in

2. In the second line, undivided, we see its subject as the dragon appearing in the field. It will be advantageous to meet with the great man.

3. In the third line, undivided, we see its subject as the superior man active and vigilant all the day, and in the evening still careful and apprehensive. The position is dangerous, but there will be no mistake.

4. In the fourth line, undivided, we see its subject as the dragon looking as if he were leaping up, but still in the deep. There will be no mistake.

5. In the fifth line, undivided, we see its subject as the dragon on the wing in the sky. It will be advantageous to meet with the great man.

6. In the sixth or topmost line, undivided, we see its subject as the dragon exceeding the proper limits. There will be occasion for repentance.

7. The lines of this hexagram are all strong and undivided, as appears from the use of the number nine. If the host of dragons thus appearing were to divest themselves of their heads, there would be good fortune.

divination. Up and down throughout the text of the 64 hexagrams, we often find the characters thus coupled together. Both interpretations are possible. I have followed what is accepted as the view of Confucius. It would take pages to give a tithe of what has been written in justification of it, and to reconcile it with the other.

"The dragon" is the symbol employed by the Duke of Chau to represent "the superior man" and especially "the great man," exhibiting the virtues or attributes characteristic of heaven. The creature's proper home is in the water, but it can disport itself on the land, and also fly and soar aloft. It has been from the earliest time the emblem with the Chinese of the highest dignity and wisdom, of sovereignty and sagehood, the combination of which constitutes "the great man." One emblem runs through the lines of many of the hexagrams as here.

But the dragon appears in the sixth line as going beyond the proper limits. The ruling-sage has gone through all the sphere in which he is called on to display his attributes; it is time for him to relax. The line should not be always pulled tight; the bow should not be always kept drawn. The unchanging use of force will give occasion for repentance. The moral meaning found in the line is that "the high shall be abased."

Such explanations as this are given in the appendixes for every hexagram.

II. THE KWAN HEXAGRAM [2]

Khwan represents what is great and originating, pene-trating, advantageous, correct and having the firmness of a mare. When the superior man (here intended) has to make any movement, if he take the initiative, he will go astray; if he follow, he will find his proper lord. The ad-vantageousness will be seen in his getting friends in the southwest, and losing friends in the northeast. If he rest in correctness and firmness, there will be good fortune.

1. In the first line, divided, we see its subject treading on hoar frost. The strong ice will come by and by.

2. The second line, divided, shows the attribute of being straight, square, and great. Its operation, without repeated efforts, will be in every respect advantageous.

3. The third line, divided, shows its subject keeping his excellence under restraint, but firmly maintaining it. If he should have occasion to engage in the king's service, though he will not claim the success for himself, he will bring affairs to a good issue.

4. The fourth line, divided, shows the symbol of a sack tied up. There will be no ground for blame or for praise.

5. The fifth line, divided, shows the yellow lower gar-ment. There will be great good fortune.

6. The sixth line, divided, shows dragons fighting in the wild. Their blood is purple and yellow.

7. The lines of this hexagram are all weak and divided,

[2] The same attributes are here ascribed to *Khwan*, as in the former hexagram to Chien; but with a difference. The figure, made up of six divided lines, expresses the ideal of subordination and docility. The superior man, represented by it, must not take the initiative; and by following he will find his lord — the subject, that is, of Chien. Again, the correctness and firmness is defined to be that of " a mare," " docile and strong," but a creature for the service of man. That it is not the sex of the animal which the writer has chiefly in mind is plain from the immediate mention of the superior man, and his lord.

as appears from the use of the number six. If those who are thus represented be perpetually correct and firm, advantage will arise.

III. The Chun Hexagram [3]

Chun indicates that in the case which it presupposes there will be great progress and success, and the advantage will come from being correct and firm. But any movement in advance should not be lightly undertaken. There will be advantage in appointing feudal princes.

1. The first line, undivided, shows the difficulty its subject has in advancing. It will be advantageous for him to abide correct and firm; advantageous also to be made a feudal ruler.

2. The second line, divided, shows its subject distressed and obliged to return; even the horses of her chariot also seem to be retreating. But not by a spoiler is she assailed, but by one who seeks her to be his wife. The young lady maintains her firm correctness, and declines a union. After ten years she will be united, and have children.

3. The third line, divided, shows one following the deer without the guidance of the forester, and only finding himself in the midst of the forest. The superior man, acquainted with the secret risks, thinks it better to give up the chase. If he went forward, he would regret it.

4. The fourth line, divided, shows its subject as a lady, the horses of whose chariot appear in retreat. She seeks, however, the help of him who seeks her to be his wife. Advance will be fortunate; all will turn out advantageously.

[3] The character called *Chun* is pictorial, and was intended to show us how a plant struggles with difficulty out of the earth, rising gradually above the surface. This difficulty, marking the first stages in the growth of a plant, is used to symbolize the struggles that mark the rise of a State out of a condition of disorder, consequent on a great revolution.

5. The fifth line, undivided, shows the difficulties in the way of its subject's dispensing the rich favors that might be expected from him. With firmness and correctness there will be good fortune in small things; even with them in great things there will be evil.

6. The topmost line, divided, shows its subject with the horses of his chariot obliged to retreat, and weeping tears of blood in streams.

IV. THE MANG HEXAGRAM [4]

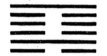

Mang indicates that in the case which it presupposes there will be progress and success. I do not go and seek the youthful and inexperienced, but he comes and seeks me. When he shows the sincerity that marks the first recourse to divination, I instruct him. If he apply a second and third time, that is troublesome; and I do not instruct the troublesome. There will be advantage in being firm and correct.

1. The first line, divided, has respect to the dispelling of ignorance. It will be advantageous to use punishment for that purpose, and to remove the shackles from the mind. But going on in that way of punishment will give occasion for regret.

2. The second line, undivided, shows its subject exercising forbearance with the ignorant, in which there will be good fortune; and admitting even the goodness of women,

---

[4] As *Chun* shows us plants struggling from beneath the surface, *Mang* suggests to us the small and undeveloped appearance which they then present; and hence it came to be the symbol of youthful inexperience and ignorance. The object of the hexagram is to show how such a condition should be dealt with by the parent and ruler, whose authority and duty are represented by the second and sixth, the two undivided lines. All between the first and last sentences of the *Thwan* must be taken as an oracular response received by the party divining on the subject of enlightening the youthful ignorant. This accounts for its being more than usually enigmatical, and for its being partly rhythmical.

which will also be fortunate. He may be described also as a son able to sustain the burden of his family.

3. The third line, divided, seems to say that one should not marry a woman whose emblem it might be, for that, when she sees a man of wealth, she will not keep her person from him, and in no wise will advantage come from her.

4. The fourth line, divided, shows its subject as if bound in chains of ignorance. There will be occasion for regret.

5. The fifth line, divided, shows its subject as a simple lad without experience. There will be good fortune.

6. In the topmost line, undivided, we see one smiting the ignorant youth. But no advantage will come from doing him an injury. Advantage would come from warding off injury from him.

V. THE HSU HEXAGRAM [5]

Hsu intimates that, with the sincerity which is declared in it, there will be brilliant success. With firmness there will be good fortune; and it will be advantageous to cross the great stream.

1. The first line, undivided, shows its subject waiting in

[5] *Hsu* means waiting. Strength confronted by peril might be expected to advance boldly and at once to struggle with it; but it takes the wiser plan of waiting till success is sure. This is the lesson of the hexagram. That "sincerity is declared in it" is proved from the fifth line in the position of honor and authority, central, itself undivided and in an odd place. In such a case, nothing but firm correctness is necessary to great success.

"Going through a great stream," an expression frequent in the Yi, may mean undertaking hazardous enterprises, or encountering great difficulties, without any special reference; but more natural is it to understand by "the great stream" the Yellow river, which the lords of Chau must cross in a revolutionary movement against the dynasty of Yin and its tyrant. The passage of it by King Wu, the son of Wan, in 1122 B.C., was certainly one of the greatest deeds in the history of China. It was preceded also by long "waiting," till the time of assured success came.

the distant border. It will be well for him constantly to maintain the purpose thus shown, in which case there will be no error.

2. The second line, undivided, shows its subject waiting on the sand of the mountain stream. He will suffer the small injury of being spoken against, but in the end there will be good fortune.

3. The third line, undivided, shows its subject in the mud close by the stream. He thereby invites the approach of injury.

4. The fourth line, divided, shows its subject waiting in the place of blood. But he will get out of the cavern.

5. The fifth line, undivided, shows its subject waiting amidst the appliances of a feast. Through his firmness and correctness there will be good fortune.

6. The topmost line, divided, shows its subject entered into the cavern. But there are three guests coming, without being urged, to his help. If he receive them respectfully, there will be good fortune in the end.

VI. The Sung Hexagram [6]

Sung intimates how, though there is sincerity in one's contention, he will yet meet with opposition and obstruction;

[6] We have strength in the upper trigram, as if to regulate and control the lower, and peril in that lower as if looking out for an opportunity to assail the upper; or, as it may be represented, we have one's self in a state of peril matched against strength from without. All this is supposed to give the idea of contention or strife. But the undivided line in the center of *Khan* is emblematic of sincerity, and gives a character to the whole figure. An individual, so represented, will be very wary, and have good fortune; but strife is bad, and, if persevered in even by such a one, the effect will be evil. The fifth line, undivided, in an odd place, and central, serves as a representative of "the great man," whose agency is sure to be good; but the topmost line being also strong, and with its two companions, riding as it were, on the trigram of peril, its action is likely to be too rash for a great enterprise.

but if he cherish an apprehensive caution, there will be good fortune, while, if he must prosecute the contention to the bitter end, there will be evil.   It will be advantageous to see the great man; it will not be advantageous to cross the great stream.

1. The first line, divided, shows its subject not perpetuating the matter about which the contention is.   He will suffer the small injury of being spoken against, but the end will be fortunate.

2. The second line, undivided, shows its subject unequal to the contention.   If he retire and keep concealed where the inhabitants of his city are only three hundred families, he will fall into no mistake.

3. The third line, divided, shows its subject keeping in the old place assigned for his support, and firmly correct. Perilous as the position is, there will be good fortune in the end.   Should he perchance engage in the king's business, he will not claim the merit of achievement.

4. The fourth line, undivided, shows its subject unequal to the contention.   He returns to the study of Heaven's ordinances, changes his wish to contend, and rests in being firm and correct.   There will be good fortune.

5. The fifth line, undivided, shows its subject contending — and with great good fortune.

6. The topmost line, undivided, shows how its subject may have the leathern belt conferred on him by the sovereign, and thrice it shall be taken from him in a morning.

VII.   THE SZE HEXAGRAM [7]

Sze indicates how, in the case which it supposes, with firmness and correctness, and a leader of age and experience, there will be good fortune and no error.

[7] The conduct of military expeditions in a feudal kingdom, and we may say, generally, is denoted by the hexagram *Sze*.

1. The first line, divided, shows the host going forth according to the rules for such a movement. If these be not good, there will be evil.

2. The second line, undivided, shows the leader in the midst of the host. There will be good fortune and no error. The king has thrice conveyed to him the orders of his favor.

3. The third line, divided, shows how the host may, possibly, have many inefficient leaders. There will be evil.

4. The fourth line, divided, shows the host in retreat. There is no error.

5. The fifth line, divided, shows birds in the fields, which it will be advantageous to seize and destroy. In that case there will be no error. If the oldest son leads the host, the younger men idly occupy offices assigned to them, however firm and correct he may be, there will be evil.

6. The topmost line, divided, shows the great ruler delivering his charges, appointing some to be rulers of States, and others to undertake the headship of clans; but small men should not be employed in such positions.

VIII. THE PI HEXAGRAM [8]

Pi indicates that under the conditions which it supposes there is good fortune. But let the principal party intended in it reexamine himself, as if by divination, whether his virtue be great, unintermitting, and firm. If it be so, there will be no error. Those who have not rest will then come to him; and with those who are too late in coming it will be ill.

1. The first line, divided, shows its subject seeking by

[8] The idea of union between the different members and classes of a State, and how it can be secured, is the subject of the hexagram *Pi*. The whole line occupying the fifth place, or that of authority, in the hexagram, represents the ruler to whom the subjects of all the other lines offer a ready submission.

his sincerity to win the attachment of his object. There will be no error. Let the breast be full of sincerity as an earthenware vessel is of its contents, and it will in the end bring other advantages.

2. In the second line, divided, we see the movement toward union and attachment proceeding from the inward mind. With firm correctness there will be good fortune.

3. In the third line, divided, we see its subject seeking for union with such as ought not to be associated with.

4. In the fourth line, divided, we see its subject seeking for union with the one beyond himself. With firm correctness there will be good fortune.

5. The fifth line, undivided, affords the most illustrious instance of seeking union and attachment. We seem to see in it the king urging his pursuit of the game only in three directions, and allowing the escape of all the animals before him, while the people of his towns do not warn one another to prevent it. There will be good fortune.

6. In the topmost line, divided, we see one seeking union and attachment without having taken the first step to such an end. There will be evil.

IX. The Hsiao Chu Hexagram[9]

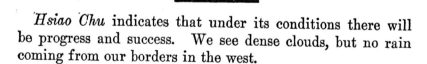

Hsiao Chu indicates that under its conditions there will be progress and success. We see dense clouds, but no rain coming from our borders in the west.

[9] The name *Hsiao Chu* is interpreted as meaning "small restraint." The idea of "restraint" having once been determined on as that to be conveyed by the figure, it is easily made out that the restraint must be small, for its representative is the divided line in the fourth place; and the check given by that to all the undivided lines can not be great. Even if we suppose, as many critics do, that all the virtue of that upper trigram *Sun* is concentrated in its first line, the attribute ascribed to *Sun* is that of docile flexibility, which can not long be successful against the strength emblemed by the lower trigram *Chien*. The restraint therefore is small, and in the end there will be "progress and success."

The second sentence of the *Thwan* contains indications of the place,

1. The first line, undivided, shows its subject returning and pursuing his own course. What mistake should he fall into? There will be good fortune.

2. The second line, undivided, shows its subject, by the attraction of the former line, returning to the proper course. There will be good fortune.

3. The third line, undivided, suggests the idea of a carriage, the strap beneath which has been removed, or of a husband and wife looking on each other with averted eyes.

4. The fourth line, divided, shows its subject possessed of sincerity. The danger of bloodshed is thereby averted, and his ground for apprehension dismissed. There will be no mistake.

5. The fifth line, undivided, shows its subject possessed of sincerity, and drawing others to unite with him. Rich in resources, he employs his neighbors in the same cause with himself.

6. The topmost line, undivided, shows how the rain has fallen, and the onward progress is stayed; — so must we value the full accumulation of the virtue, represented by the upper trigram. But a wife exercising restraint, however firm and correct she may be, is in a position of peril, and like the moon approaching to the full. If the superior man prosecute his measures in such circumstances, there will be evil.

time, and personality of the writer which it seems possible to ascertain. The fief of Chau was the western portion of the kingdom of Yin or Shang, the China of the twelfth century B.C., the era of King Wan. Rain coming and moistening the ground is the cause of the beauty and luxuriance of the vegetable world; and the emblem of the blessings flowing from good training and good government. Here therefore in the west, the hereditary territory of the house of Chau, are blessings which might enrich the whole kingdom; but they are somehow restrained. The dense clouds do not empty their stores.

Regis says: "To declare openly that no rain fell from the heavens long covered with dense clouds over the great tract of country, which stretched from the western border to the court and on to the eastern sea, was nothing else but leaving it to all thoughtful minds to draw the conclusion that the family of Wan was as worthy of the supreme seat as that of Shau, the tyrant, however ancient, was unworthy of it." The intimation is not put in the text, however, so clearly as by Regis.

X. THE LI HEXAGRAM [10]

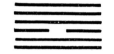

Li suggests the idea of one treading on the tail of a tiger, which does not bite him. There will be progress and success.

1. The first line, undivided, shows its subject treading his accustomed path. If he go forward, there will be no error.

2. The second line, undivided, shows its subject treading the path that is level and easy; a quiet and solitary man, to whom, if he be firm and correct, there will be good fortune.

3. The third line, divided, shows a one-eyed man who thinks he can see; a lame man who thinks he can walk well; one who treads on the tail of a tiger and is bitten. All this indicates ill fortune. We have a mere bravo acting the part of a great ruler.

4. The fourth line, undivided, shows its subject treading on the tail of a tiger. He becomes full of apprehensive caution, and in the end there will be good fortune.

5. The fifth line, undivided, shows the resolute tread of its subject. Though he be firm and correct, there will be peril.

6. The sixth line, undivided, tells us to look at the whole course that is trodden, and examine the presage which that gives. If it be complete and without failure, there will be great good fortune.

[10] The character giving its name to the hexagram plays an important part also in the symbolism; and this may be the reason why it does not, as the name, occupy the first place in the *Thwan*. Looking at the figure, we see it is made up of the trigrams *Tui*, representing a marsh, and *Chien*, representing the sky. *Tui* is a *yin* trigram, and its top line is divided. Below *Chien*, the great symbol of strength, it may readily suggest the idea of treading on a tiger's tail, which was an old way of expressing what was hazardous (Shu V, xxv, 2). But what suggests the statement that "the tiger does not bite the treader"? The attribute of *Tui* is "pleased satisfaction." Of course such an attribute could not be predicated of one who was in the fangs of a tiger. The coming scatheless out of such danger further suggests the idea of "progress and success."

XI. The Thai Hexagram [11]

In *Thai* we see the little gone and the great come. It indicates that there will be good fortune, with progress and success.

1. The first line, undivided, suggests the idea of grass pulled up, and bringing with it other stalks with whose roots it is connected. Advance on the part of its subject will be fortunate.

2. The second line, undivided, shows one who can bear with the uncultivated, will cross the Ho without a boat, does not forget the distant, and has no selfish friendships. Thus does he prove himself acting in accordance with the course of the due Mean.

3. The third line, undivided, shows that, while there is no state of peace that is not liable to be disturbed, and no departure of evil men so that they shall not return, yet when one is firm and correct, as he realizes the distresses that may arise, he will commit no error. There is no occasion for sadness at the certainty of such recurring changes; and in this mood the happiness of the present may be long enjoyed.

4. The fourth line, divided, shows its subject fluttering down; — not relying on his own rich resources, but calling in his neighbors. They all come not as having received warning, but in the sincerity of their hearts.

5. The fifth line, divided, reminds us of King Ti-yi's rule

[11] The language of the *Thwan* has reference to the form of *Thai*, with the three strong lines of *Chien* below, and the three weak lines of *Khwan* above. The former are "the great," active and vigorous; the latter are "the small," inactive and submissive. A course in which the motive forces are represented by the three strong, and the opposing by the three weak lines, must be progressive and successful. *Thai* is called the hexagram of the first month of the year, the first month of the natural spring, when for six months, through the fostering sun and genial skies, the processes of growth will be going on.

about the marriage of his younger sister. By such a course there is happiness and there will be great good fortune.

6. The sixth line, divided, shows us the city wall returned into the moat. It is not the time to use the army. The subject of the line may, indeed, announce his orders to the people of his own city; but however correct and firm he may be, he will have cause for regret.

XII. The Phi Hexagram [12]

In *Phi* there is the want of good understanding between the different classes of men, and its indication is unfavorable to the firm and correct course of the superior man. We see in it the great gone and the little come.

1. The first line, divided, suggests the idea of grass pulled up, and bringing with it other stalks with whose roots it is connected. With firm correctness on the part of its subject, there will be good fortune and progress.

2. The second line, divided, shows its subject patient and obedient. To the small man comporting himself so there will be good fortune. If the great man comport himself as the distress and obstruction require, he will have success.

3. The third line, divided, shows its subject ashamed of the purpose folded in his breast.

4. The fourth line, undivided, shows its subject acting in accordance with the ordination of Heaven, and committing no error. His companions will come and share in his happiness.

5. In the fifth line, undivided, we see him who brings the distress and obstruction to a close — the great man and for-

---

[12] The form of *Phi*, it will be seen, is exactly the opposite of that of *Thai*. Much of what has been said on the interpretation of that will apply to this, or at least assist the student in making out the meaning of its symbolism. *Phi* is the hexagram of the seventh month. Genial influences have done their work, the processes of growth are at an end. Henceforth increasing decay must be looked for.

tunate. But let him say, "We may perish! We may perish!" so shall the state of things become firm, as if bound to a clump of bushy mulberry-trees.

6. The sixth line, undivided, shows the overthrow and removal of the condition of distress and obstruction. Before this there was that condition. Hereafter there will be joy.

XIII. THE THUNG TSAN HEXAGRAM [13]

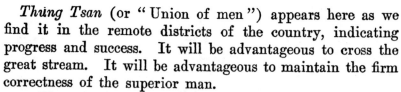

Thung Tsan (or "Union of men") appears here as we find it in the remote districts of the country, indicating progress and success. It will be advantageous to cross the great stream. It will be advantageous to maintain the firm correctness of the superior man.

1. The first line, undivided, shows the representative of the union of men just issuing from his gate. There will be no error.

2. The second line, divided, shows the representative of the union of men just issuing from his gate. There will be occasion for regret.

3. The third line, undivided, shows its subject with his arms hidden in the thick grass, and at the top of a high mound. But for three years he makes no demonstration.

[13] *Thung Tsan* describes a condition of nature and of the state opposite to that of *Phi*. There were distress and obstruction; here is union. But the union must be based entirely on public considerations, without taint of selfishness.

The strong line in the fifth, its correct, place, occupies the most important position, and has for its correlate the weak second line, also in its correct place. The one divided line is naturally sought after by all the strong lines. The upper trigram is that of heaven, which is above; the lower is that of fire, whose tendency is to mount upward. All these things are in harmony with the idea of union. But the union must be free from all selfish motives, and this is indicated by its being in the remote districts of the country, where people are unsophisticated, and free from the depraving effects incident to large societies. A union from such motives will cope with the greatest difficulties; and yet a word of caution is added.

4. The fourth line, undivided, shows its subject mounted on the city wall; but he does not proceed to make the attack he contemplates. There will be good fortune.

5. In the fifth line, undivided, the representative of the union of men first wails and cries out, and then laughs. His great host conquers, and he and the subject of the second line meet together.

6. The topmost line, undivided, shows the representative of the union of men in the suburbs. There will be no occasion for repentance.

XIV.   The Ta Yu Hexagram [14]

Ta Yu indicates that, under the circumstances which it implies, there will be great progress and success.

1. In the first line, undivided, there is no approach to what is injurious, and there is no error. Let there be a realization of the difficulty and danger of the position, and there will be no error to the end.

2. In the second line, undivided, we have a large wagon with its load. In whatever direction advance is made, there will be no error.

3. The third line, undivided, shows us a feudal prince presenting his offerings to the Son of Heaven. A small man would be unequal to such a duty.

4. The fourth line, undivided, shows its subject keeping his great resources under restraint. There will be no error.

5. The fifth line, divided, shows the sincerity of its sub-

[14] *Ta Yu* means " Great Havings "; denoting in a kingdom a state of prosperity and abundance, and in a family or individual, a state of opulence. The danger threatening such a condition arises from the pride which it is likely to engender. But everything here is against that issue. Apart from the symbolism of the trigrams, we have the place of honor occupied by a weak line, so that its subject will be humble; and all the other lines, strong as they are, will act in obedient sympathy. There will be great progress and success.

ject reciprocated by that of all the others represented in the hexagram. Let him display a proper majesty, and there will be good fortune.

6. The topmost line, undivided, shows its subject with help accorded to him from Heaven. There will be good fortune, advantage in every respect.

XV. THE CHIEN HEXAGRAM [15]

Chien indicates progress and success. The superior man, being humble as it implies, will have a good issue to his undertakings.

1. The first line, divided, shows us the superior man who adds humility to humility. Even the great stream may be crossed with this, and there will be good fortune.

2. The second line, divided, shows us humility that has made itself recognized. With firm correctness there will be good fortune.

3. The third line, undivided, shows the superior man of acknowledged merit. He will maintain his success to the end, and have good fortune.

4. The fourth line, divided, shows one, whose action would be in every way advantageous, stirring up the more his humility.

5. The fifth line, divided, shows one who, without being rich, is able to employ his neighbors. He may advantageously use the force of arms. All his movements will be advantageous.

6. The sixth line, divided, shows us humility that has made itself recognized. The subject of it will with advan-

---

[15] An essay on humility rightly follows that on abundant possessions. The third line, which is a whole line amid five others divided, occupying the topmost place in the lower trigram, is held by the Khang-hsi editors and many others to be " the lord of the hexagram," the representative of humility, strong, but abasing itself.

tage put his hosts in motion; but he will only punish his own towns and State.

XVI. THE YU HEXAGRAM [16]

Yu indicates that, in the State which it implies, feudal princes may be set up, and the hosts put in motion, with advantage.

1. The first line, divided, shows its subject proclaiming his pleasure and satisfaction. There will be evil.

2. The second line, divided, shows one who is firm as a rock. He sees a thing without waiting till it has come to pass; with his firm correctness there will be good fortune.

3. The third line, divided, shows one looking up for favors, while he indulges the feeling of pleasure and satisfaction. If he would understand! — If he be late in doing so, there will indeed be occasion for repentance.

4. The fourth line, undivided, shows him from whom the harmony and satisfaction come. Great is the success which he obtains. Let him not allow suspicions to enter his mind, and thus friends will gather around him.

5. The fifth line, divided, shows one with a chronic complaint, but who lives on without dying.

6. The topmost line, divided, shows its subject with darkened mind devoted to the pleasure and satisfaction of the time; but if he change his course even when it may be considered as completed, there will be no error.

[16] The *Yu* hexagram denoted to King Wan a condition of harmony and happy contentment throughout the kingdom, when the people rejoiced in and readily obeyed their sovereign. At such a time his appointments and any military undertakings would be hailed and supported. The fourth line, undivided, is the lord of the figure, and, being close to the fifth or place of dignity, is to be looked on as the minister or chief officer of the ruler. The ruler gives to him his confidence; and all represented by the other lines yield their obedience.

XVII. THE SUI HEXAGRAM [17]

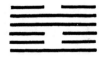

Sui indicates that under its conditions there will be great progress and success. But it will be advantageous to be firm and correct. There will then be no error.

1. The first line, undivided, shows us one changing the object of his pursuit; but if he be firm and correct, there will be good fortune. Going beyond his own gate to find associates, he will achieve merit.

2. The second line, divided, shows us one who cleaves to the little boy, and lets go the man of age and experience.

3. The third line, divided, shows us one who cleaves to the man of age and experience, and lets go the little boy. Such following will get what it seeks; but it will be advantageous to adhere to what is firm and correct.

4. The fourth line, undivided, shows us one followed and obtaining adherents. Though he be firm and correct, there will be evil. If he be sincere, however, in his course, and make that evident, into what error will he fall?

5. The fifth line, undivided, shows us the ruler sincere in fostering all that is excellent. There will be good fortune.

6. The topmost line, divided, shows us that sincerity firmly held and clung to, yea, and bound fast. We see the king with it presenting his offerings on the western mountain.

---

[17] *Sui* symbolizes the idea of "following." It is said to follow *Yu*, the symbol of harmony and satisfaction. Where there are these conditions men are sure to follow; nor will they follow those in whom they have no complacency. The hexagram includes the cases where one follows others, and where others follow him; and the auspice of great progress and success is due to this flexibility and applicability of it. But in both cases the following must be guided by a reference to what is proper and correct.

XVIII. The Ku Hexagram [18]

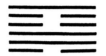

Ku indicates great progress and success to him who deals properly with the condition represented by it. There will be advantage in efforts like that of crossing the great stream. He should weigh well, however, the events of three days before the turning point, and those to be done three days after it.

1. The first line, divided, shows a son dealing with the troubles caused by his father. If he be an able son, the father will escape the blame of having erred. The position is perilous, but there will be good fortune in the end.

2. The second line, undivided, shows a son dealing with the troubles caused by his mother. He should not carry his firm correctness to the utmost.

3. The third line, undivided, shows a son dealing with the troubles caused by his father. There may be some small occasion for repentance, but there will not be any great error.

4. The fourth line, divided, shows a son viewing indulgently the troubles caused by his father. If he go forward, he will find cause to regret it.

5. The fifth line, divided, shows a son dealing with the troubles caused by his father. He obtains the praise of using the fit instrument for his work.

[18] In the 6th Appendix it is said, "They who follow another are sure to have services to perform, and hence *Sui* is followed by *Ku*." But *Ku* means the having painful or troublesome services to do. It denotes here a state in which things are going to ruin, as if through poison or venomous worms; and the figure is supposed to describe the arrest of the decay and the restoration to soundness and vigor, so as to justify its auspice of great progress and success. To realize such a result, however, great efforts will be required, as in crossing the great stream; and a careful consideration of the events that have brought on the state of decay, and the measures to be taken to remedy it, is also necessary.

6. The sixth line, undivided, shows us one who does not serve either king or feudal lord, but in a lofty spirit prefers to attend to his own affairs.

XIX. THE LIN HEXAGRAM [19]

Lin indicates that under the conditions supposed in it there will be great progress and success, while it will be advantageous to be firmly correct. In the eighth month there will be evil.

1. The first line, undivided, shows its subject advancing in company with the subject of the second line. Through his firm correctness there will be good fortune.

2. The second line, undivided, shows its subject advancing in company with the subject of the first line. There will be good fortune; advancing will be in every way advantageous.

3. The third line, divided, shows one well pleased indeed to advance, but whose action will be in no way advantageous. If he become anxious about it, however, there will be no error.

4. The fourth line, divided, shows one advancing in the highest mode. There will be no error.

5. The fifth line, divided, shows the advance of wisdom, such as befits the great ruler. There will be good fortune.

6. The sixth line, divided, shows the advance of honesty and generosity. There will be good fortune, and no error.

[19] In Appendix VI *Lin* is explained as meaning "great." *Lin* denotes the approach of authority — to inspect, to comfort, or to rule. When we look at the figure, we see two strong undivided lines advancing on the four weak lines above them, and thence follows the assurance that their action will be powerful and successful. That action must be governed by rectitude, however, and by caution grounded on the changing character of all conditions and events. The meaning of the concluding sentence is given in Appendix I as simply being — that, "the advancing power will decay in no long time."

XX. THE KWAN HEXAGRAM [20]

Kwan shows how he whom it represents should be like the worshiper who has washed his hands, but not yet presented his offerings — with sincerity and an appearance of dignity, commanding reverent regard.

1. The first line, divided, shows the looking of a lad; not blamable in men of inferior rank, but matter for regret in superior men.

2. The second line, divided, shows one peeping out from a door. It would be advantageous if it were merely the firm correctness of a female.

3. The third line, divided, shows one looking at the course of his own life, to advance or recede accordingly.

4. The fourth line, divided, shows one contemplating the glory of the kingdom. It will be advantageous for him, being such as he is, to seek to be a guest of the king.

5. The fifth line, undivided, shows its subject contemplating his own life-course. A superior man, he will thus fall into no error.

6. The sixth line, undivided, shows its subject contemplating his character to see if it be indeed that of a superior man. He will not fall into error.

[20] The Chinese character *Kwan*, from which this hexagram is named, is used in it in two senses. In the *Thwan*, the first paragraph of the treatise on the *Thwan*, and the paragraph on the Great Symbolism, it denotes " showing," " manifesting "; in all other places it denotes " contemplating," " looking at." The subject of the hexagram is the sovereign and his subjects, how he manifests himself to them, and how they contemplate him. The two upper, undivided, lines belong to the sovereign; the four weak lines below them are his subjects — ministers and others who look up at him. *Kwan* is the hexagram of the eighth month.

In the *Thwan* King Wan symbolizes the sovereign by a worshiper when he is most solemn in his religious service, at the commencement of it, full of sincerity and with a dignified carriage.

XXI. The Shih Ho Hexagram [21]

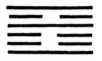

Shih Ho indicates successful progress in the condition of things which it supposes. It will be advantageous to use legal constraints.

1. The first line, undivided, shows one with his feet in the stocks and deprived of his toes. There will be no error.

2. The second line, divided, shows one biting through the soft flesh, and going on to bite off the nose. There will be no error.

3. The third line, divided, shows one gnawing dried flesh, and meeting with what is disagreeable. There will be occasion for some small regret, but no great error.

4. The fourth line, undivided, shows one gnawing the flesh dried on the bone, and getting the pledges of money and arrows. It will be advantageous to him to realize the difficulty of his task and be firm; in which case there will be good fortune.

5. The fifth line, divided, shows one gnawing at dried flesh, and finding the yellow gold. Let him be firm and correct, realizing the peril of his position. There will be no error.

6. The sixth line, undivided, shows one wearing the cangue, and deprived of his ears. There will be evil.

[21] *Shih Ho* means, literally, "Union by gnawing." We see in the figure two strong lines in the first and last places, while all the others, with the exception of the fourth, are divided. This suggests the idea of the jaws and the mouth between them kept open by something in it. Let that be gnawed through and the mouth will close and the jaws come together. So in the body politic. Remove the obstacles to union, and high and low will come together with a good understanding. And how are those obstacles to be removed? By force, emblemed by the gnawing; that is, by legal constraints. And these are sure to be successful. The auspice of the figure is favorable. There will be success.

XXII. THE PI HEXAGRAM[22]

Pi indicates that there should be free course in what it denotes. There will be little advantage, however, if it be allowed to advance and take the lead.

1. The first line, undivided, shows one adorning the way of his feet. He can discard a carriage and walk on foot.

2. The second line, divided, shows one adorning his beard.

3. The third line, undivided, shows its subject with the appearance of being adorned and bedewed with rich favors. But let him ever maintain his firm correctness, and there will be good fortune.

4. The fourth line, divided, shows one looking as if adorned, but only in white. As if mounted on a white horse, and furnished with wings, he seeks union with the subject of the first line, while the intervening third pursues, not as a robber, but intent on a matrimonial alliance.

5. The fifth line, divided, shows its subject adorned by the occupants of the heights and gardens. He bears his roll of silk, small and slight. He may appear stingy; but there will be good fortune in the end.

6. The sixth line, undivided, shows one with white as his only ornament. There will be no error.

[22] The character *Pi* is the symbol of what is ornamental and of the act of adorning. As there is ornament in nature, so should there be in society; but its place is secondary to that of what is substantial. This is the view of King Wan in his *Thwan*. The symbolism of the separate lines is sometimes fantastic.

XXIII. The Po Hexagram [23]

Po indicates that in the state which it symbolizes it will not be advantageous to make a movement in any direction whatever.

1. The first line, divided, shows one overturning the couch by injuring its legs. The injury will go on to the destruction of all firm correctness, and there will be evil.

2. The second line, divided, shows one overthrowing the couch by injuring its frame. The injury will go on to the destruction of all firm correctness, and there will be evil.

3. The third line, divided, shows its subject among the overthrowers; but there will be no error.

4. The fourth line, divided, shows its subject having overthrown the couch, and going to injure the skin of him who lies on it. There will be evil.

5. The fifth line, divided, shows its subject leading on the others like a string of fishes, and obtaining for them the favor that lights on the inmates of the palace. There will be advantage in every way.

6. The topmost line, undivided, shows its subject as a great fruit which has not been eaten. The superior man finds the people again as a chariot carrying him. The small men by their course overthrow their own dwellings.

[23] *Po* is the symbol of falling or of causing to fall, and may be applied, both in the natural and political world, to the process of decay, or that of overthrow. The figure consists of five divided lines, and one undivided, which last thus becomes the prominent and principal line in the figure. Decay or overthrow has begun at the bottom of it, and crept up to the top. The hexagram is that of the ninth month, when the beauty and glory of summer have disappeared, and the year is ready to fall into the arms of sterile winter. In the political world, small men have gradually displaced good men and great, till but one remains; and the lesson for him is to wait. The power operating against him is too strong; but the fashion of political life passes away. If he wait, a change for the better will shortly appear.

The lesser symbolism is chiefly that of a bed or couch with its

XXIV. THE FU HEXAGRAM [24]

Fu indicates that there will be free course and progress in what it denotes. The subject of it finds no one to distress him in his exits and entrances; friends come to him, and no error is committed. He will return and repeat his proper course. In seven days comes his return. There will be advantage in whatever direction movement is made.

1. The first line, undivided, shows its subject returning from an error of no great extent, which would not proceed to anything requiring repentance. There will be great good fortune.

occupant. The idea of the hexagram requires this occupant to be overthrown, or at least that an attempt be made to overthrow him. Accordingly the attempt in line 1 is made by commencing with the legs of the couch. The symbolism goes on to explain itself. The object of the evil worker is the overthrow of all firm correctness. Of course there will be evil.

[24] *Fu* symbolizes the idea of returning, coming back or over again. The last hexagram showed us inferior prevailing over superior men, all that is good in nature and society yielding before what is bad. But change is the law of nature and society. When decay has reached its climax, recovery will begin to take place. In *Po* we had one strong topmost line, and five weak lines below it; here we have one strong line, and five weak lines above it. To illustrate the subject from what we see in nature, *Po* is the hexagram of the ninth month, in which the triumph of cold and decay in the year is nearly complete. It is complete in the tenth month, whose hexagram is *Khwan;* then follows our hexagram *Fu*, belonging to the eleventh month, in which was the winter solstice when the sun turned back in his course, and moved with a constant regular progress toward the summer solstice. In harmony with these changes of nature are the changes in the political and social state of a nation. There is nothing in the *Yi* to suggest the hope of a perfect society or kingdom that can not be moved.

The strong bottom line is the first of *Chan*, the trigram of movement, and the upper trigram is *Khwan*, denoting docility and capacity. The strong returning line will meet with no distressing obstacle, and the weak lines will change before it into strong, and be as friends. The bright quality will be developed brighter and brighter from day to day, and month to month.

2. The second line, divided, shows the admirable return of its subject. There will be good fortune.

3. The third line, divided, shows one who has made repeated returns. The position is perilous, but there will be no error.

4. The fourth line, divided, shows its subject moving right in the center among those represented by the other divided lines, and yet returning alone to his proper path.

5. The fifth line, divided, shows the noble return of its subject. There will be no ground for repentance.

6. The topmost line, divided, shows its subject all astray on the subject of returning. There will be evil. There will be calamities and errors. If with his views he put the hosts in motion, the end will be a great defeat, whose issues will extend to the ruler of the State. Even in ten years he will not be able to repair the disaster.

XXV. The Wu Wang Hexagram [25]

Wu Wang indicates great progress and success, while there will be advantage in being firm and correct. If its subject and his action be not correct, he will fall into errors, and it will not be advantageous for him to move in any direction.

1. The first line, undivided, shows its subject free from all insincerity. His advance will be accompanied with good fortune.

2. The second line, divided, shows one who reaps without

[25] *Wang* is the symbol of being reckless, and often of being insincere; *Wu Wang* is descriptive of a state of entire freedom from such a condition; its subject is one who is entirely simple and sincere. The quality is characteristic of the action of Heaven, and of the highest style of humanity. In this hexagram we have an essay on this noble attribute. An absolute rectitude is essential to it. The nearer one comes to the ideal of the quality, the more powerful will be his influence, the greater his success. But let him see to it that he never swerve from being correct.

having plowed that he might reap, and gathers the produce of his third year's fields without having cultivated them the first year for that end. To such a one there will be advantage in whatever direction he may move.

3. The third line, divided, shows calamity happening to one who is free from insincerity; as in the case of an ox that has been tied up. A passerby finds it and carries it off, while the people in the neighborhood have the calamity of being accused and apprehended.

4. The fourth line, undivided, shows a case in which, if its subject can remain firm and correct, there will be no error.

5. The fifth line, undivided, shows one who is free from insincerity, and yet has fallen ill. Let him not use medicine, and he will have occasion for joy in his recovery.

6. The topmost line, undivided, shows its subject free from insincerity, yet sure to fall into error, if he take action. His action will not be advantageous in any way.

XXVI. The Ta Chu Hexagram [26]

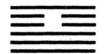

Under the conditions of *Ta Chu* it will be advantageous to be firm and correct. If its subject do not seek to enjoy his revenues in his own family without taking service at court,

[26] *Chu* has two meanings. It is the symbol of restraint, and of accumulation. What is repressed and restrained accumulates its strength and increases its volume. Both these meanings are found in the treatise on the *Thwan;* the exposition of the Great Symbolism has for its subject the accumulation of virtue. The different lines are occupied with the repression or restraint of movement. The first three lines receive that repression, the upper three exercise it. The accumulation to which all tends is that of virtue; and hence the name of *Ta Chu,* "the Great Accumulation."

What the *Thwan* teaches is that he who goes about to accumulate his virtue must be firm and correct, and may then, engaging in the public service, enjoy the king's grace, and undertake the most difficult enterprises.

there will be good fortune.   It will be advantageous for him to cross the great stream.

1. The first line, undivided, shows its subject in a position of peril.   It will be advantageous for him to stop his advance.

2. The second line, undivided, shows a carriage with the strap under it removed.

3. The third line, undivided, shows its subject urging his way with good horses.   It will be advantageous for him to realize the difficulty of his course, and to be firm and correct, exercising himself daily in his charioteering and methods of defense; then there will be advantage in whatever direction he may advance.

4. The fourth line, divided, shows the young bull, and yet having the piece of wood over his horns.   There will be great good fortune.

5. The fifth line, divided, shows the teeth of a castrated hog.   There will be good fortune.

6. The sixth line, undivided, shows its subject as in command of the firmament of heaven.   There will be progress.

XXVII.   The I Hexagram [27]

I indicates that with firm correctness there will be good fortune in what is denoted by it.   We must look at what

[27] *I* is the symbol of the upper jaw, and gives name to the hexagram; but the whole figure suggests the appearance of the mouth. There are the two undivided lines at the bottom and top, and the four divided lines between them. The first line is the first in the trigram *Chan*, denoting movement; and the sixth is the third in *Kan*, denoting what is solid. The former is the lower jaw, part of the mobile chin; and the other the more fixed upper jaw. The open lines are the cavity of the mouth. As the name of the hexagram, *I* denotes nourishing — one's body or mind, one's self or others. The nourishment in both the matter and method will differ according to the object of it; and every one must determine what to employ and do in every case by exercising his own thoughts, only one thing being promised — that in both respects the nourishing must be correct, and in

we are seeking to nourish, and by the exercise of our thoughts seek for the proper aliment.

1. The first line, undivided, seems to be thus addressed, " You leave your efficacious tortoise, and look at me till your lower jaw hangs down." There will be evil.

2. The second line, divided, shows one looking downward for nourishment, which is contrary to what is proper; or seeking it from the height above, advance toward which will lead to evil.

3. The third line, divided, shows one acting contrary to the method of nourishing. However firm he may be, there will be evil. For ten years let him not take any action, for it will not be in any way advantageous.

4. The fourth line, divided, shows one looking downward for the power to nourish. There will be good fortune. Looking with a tiger's downward unwavering glare, and with his desire that impels him to spring after spring, he will fall into no error.

5. The fifth line, divided, shows one acting contrary to what is regular and proper; but if he abide in firmness, there will be good fortune. He should not, however, try to cross the great stream.

6. The sixth line, undivided, shows him from whom comes the nourishing. His position is perilous, but there will be good fortune. It will be advantageous to cross the great stream.

XVIII. THE TA KWO HEXAGRAM [28]

Ta Kwo suggests to us a beam that is weak. There will be advantage in moving under its conditions in any direction whatever; there will be success.

harmony with what is right. The auspice of the whole hexagram is good.

[28] Very extraordinary times require very extraordinary gifts in

1. The first line, divided, shows one placing mats of the white *mao* grass under things set on the ground. There will be no error.

2. The second line, undivided, shows a decayed willow producing shoots, or an old husband in possession of his young wife. There will be advantage in every way.

3. The third line, undivided, shows a beam that is weak. There will be evil.

4. The fourth line, undivided, shows a beam curving upward. There will be good fortune. If the subject of it looks for other help but that of line one, there will be cause for regret.

5. The fifth line, undivided, shows a decayed willow producing flowers, or an old wife in possession of her young husband. There will be occasion neither for blame nor for praise.

6. The topmost line, divided, shows its subject with extraordinary boldness wading through a stream, till the water hides the crown of his head. There will be evil, but no ground for blame.

XXIX. The Khan Hexagram [29]

Khan, here repeated, shows the possession of sincerity, through which the mind is penetrating. Action in accordance with this will be of high value.

the conduct of affairs in them. This is the text on which King Wan and his son discourse after their fashion in this hexagram. What goes, in their view, to constitute anything extraordinary is its greatness and difficulty. There need not be about it what is not right.

Looking at the figure we see two weak lines at the top and bottom, and four strong lines between them, giving us the idea of a great beam unable to sustain its own weight. But the second and fifth lines are both strong and in the center; and from this and the attributes of the component trigrams a good auspice is obtained.

[29] The trigram *Khan*, which is doubled to form this hexagram, is the lineal symbol of "water." Its meaning, as a character, is "a

1. The first line, divided, shows its subject in the double defile, and yet entering a cavern within it. There will be evil.

2. The second line, undivided, shows its subject in all the peril of the defile. He will, however, get a little of the deliverance that he seeks.

3. The third line, divided, shows its subject, whether he comes or goes (*i.e.,* descends or ascends), confronted by a defile. All is peril to him and unrest. His endeavors will lead him into the cavern of the pit. There should be no action in such a case.

4. The fourth line, divided, shows its subject at a feast, with simply a bottle of spirits, and a subsidiary basket of rice, while the cups and bowls are only of earthenware. He introduces his important lessons as his ruler's intelligence admits. There will in the end be no error.

5. The fifth line, undivided, shows the water of the defile not yet full, so that it might flow away; but order will soon be brought about. There will be no error.

6. The topmost line, divided, shows its subject bound with cords of three strands or two strands, and placed in the thicket of thorns. But in three years he does not learn the course for him to pursue. There will be evil.

pit," " a perilous cavity, or defile"; and here and elsewhere in the *Yi* it leads the reader to think of a dangerous defile, with water flowing through it. It becomes symbolic of danger, and what the authors of the text had in mind was to show how danger should be encountered, its effect on the mind, and how to get out of it.

The trigram exhibits a strong central line, between two divided lines. The central represented to King Wan the sincere honesty and goodness of the subject of the hexagram, whose mind was sharpened and made penetrating by contact with danger, and who acted in a manner worthy of his character. It is implied, though the *Thwan* does not say it, that he would get out of the danger.

XXX. The Li Hexagram [30]

Li indicates that, in regard to what it denotes, it will be advantageous to be firm and correct, and that thus there will be free course and success. Let its subject also nourish a docility like that of the cow, and there will be good fortune.

1. The first line, undivided, shows one ready to move with confused steps. But he treads at the same time reverently, and there will be no mistake.

2. The second line, divided, shows its subject in his place in yellow. There will be great good fortune.

3. The third line, undivided, shows its subject in a position like that of the declining sun. Instead of playing on his instrument of earthenware, and singing to it, he utters the groans of an old man of eighty. There will be evil.

4. The fourth line, undivided, shows the manner of its subject's coming. How abrupt it is, as with fire, with death, to be rejected by all!

5. The fifth line, divided, shows its subject as one with

[30] *Li* is the name of the trigram representing fire and light, and the sun as the source of both of these. Its virtue or attribute is brightness, and by a natural metaphor intelligence. But *Li* has also the meaning of inhering in, or adhering to, being attached to. Both these significations occur in connection with the hexagram, and make it difficult to determine what was the subject of it in the minds of the authors. If we take the whole figure as expressing the subject, we have, as in the treatise on the *Thwan*, "a double brightness," a phrase which is understood to denominate the ruler. If we take the two central lines as indicating the subject, we have weakness, dwelling with strength above and below. In either case there are required from the subject a strict adherence to what is correct, and a docile humility. On the second member of the *Thwan* Chang-tze says: "The nature of the ox is docile, and that of the cow is much more so. The subject of the hexagram adhering closely to what is correct, he must be able to act in obedience to it, as docile as a cow, and then there will be good fortune."

tears flowing in torrents, and groaning in sorrow. There will be good fortune.

6. The topmost line, undivided, shows the king employing its subject in his punitive expeditions. Achieving admirable merit, he breaks only the chiefs of the rebels. Where his prisoners were not their associates, he does not punish. There will be no error.

END OF THE FIRST PART OF THE YI KING

APPENDIX V

TREATISE OF REMARKS ON THE TRIGRAMS

Chapter I. 1. Anciently, when the sages made the *Yi*, in order to give mysterious assistance to the spiritual Intelligences, they produced the rules for the use of the divining plant.

2. The number 3 was assigned to heaven, 2 to earth, and from these came the other numbers.

3. They contemplated the changes in the divided and undivided lines by the process of manipulating the stalks, and formed the trigrams; from the movements that took place in the strong and weak lines, they produced their teaching about the separate lines. There ensued a harmonious conformity to the course of duty and to virtue, with a discrimination of what was right in each particular case. They thus made an exhaustive discrimination of what was right, and effected the complete development of every nature, till they arrived in the Yi at what was appointed for it by Heaven.

Chapter II. 4. Anciently, when the sages made the Yi, it was with the design that its figures should be in conformity with the principles underlying the natures of men and things, and the ordinances for them appointed by Heaven. With this view they exhibited in them the way of heaven, calling the lines *yin* and *yang;* the way of earth, calling them the weak or soft and the strong or hard; and the way of men, under the names of benevolence and righteousness. Each trigram embraced those three Powers; and, being repeated, its full form consisted of six lines. A distinction was made of the places assigned to the *yin* and *yang* lines, which were variously occupied, now by the strong and now by the weak forms, and thus the figure of each hexagram was completed.

Chapter III. 5. The symbols of heaven and earth received

their determinate positions; those for mountains and collections of water interchanged their influences; those for thunder and wind excited each other the more; and those for water and fire did each other no harm. Then among these eight symbols there was a mutual communication.

6. The numbering of the past is a natural process; the knowledge of the coming is anticipation. Therefore in the Yi we have both anticipation and the natural process.

Chapter IV. 7. "Thunder" serves to put things in motion; "wind" to scatter the genial seeds of them; "rain" to moisten them; the "sun" to warm them; what is symbolized by *Kan,* to arrest and keep them in their places; by *Tui,* to give them joyful course; by *Chien,* to rule them; and by *Khwan,* to store them up.

Chapter V. 8.[1] God comes forth in *Chan* to his producing work; he brings his processes into full and equal action in *Sun;* they are manifested to one another in *Li;* the greatest service is done for him in *Khwan;* he rejoices in *Tui;* he struggles in *Chien;* he is comforted and enters into rest in *Khan;* and he completes the work of the year in *Kan.*

9. All things are made to issue for the *Chan,* which is placed at the east. The processes of production are brought into full and equal action in *Sun,* which is placed at the southeast. The being brought into full and equal action refers to the purity and equal arrangements of all things. *Li* gives the idea of brightness. All things are now made manifest to one another. It is the trigram of the south. The sages turn their faces to the south when they give audience

---

[1] Chapter V, paragraphs 8 and 9, sets forth the operations of nature in the various seasons, as being really the operations of God, who is named Ti, "the Lord and Ruler of Heaven." Those operations are represented in the progress by the seasons of the year, as denoted by the trigrams, according to the arrangement of them by King Wan. The "purity" predicated in paragraph 9 of things in *Sun,* was explained by Chang Khang-chang (our second century) as equivalent to "newness," referring to the brightness of all things in the light of spring and summer. On "all things receive from the earth their fullest nourishment" the same Yang, quoted above, says: "The earth performs the part of a mother. All things are its children. What a mother has to do for her children is simply to nourish them."

to all under the sky, administering government toward the region of brightness: the idea in this procedure was taken from this. *Khwan* denotes the earth, and is placed at the southwest. All things receive from it their fullest nourishment, and hence it is said, "The greatest service is done for him in *Khwan.*" *Tui* corresponds to the west and to the autumn — the season in which all things rejoice. Hence it is said, "He rejoices in *Tui.*" He struggles in *Chien,* which is the trigram of the northwest. The idea is that there the inactive and active conditions beat against each other. *Khan* denotes water. It is the trigram of the exact north — the trigram of comfort and rest, what all things are tending to. Hence it is said, "He is comforted and enters into rest in *Khan.* *Kan* is the trigram of the northeast. In it all things bring to a full end the issues of the past year, and prepare the commencement of the next. Hence it is said, "He completes the work of the year in *Kan.*"

Chapter VI. 10.[2] When we speak of Spirit we mean the subtle presence and operation of God with all things. For putting all things in motion there is nothing more vehement than thunder; for scattering them there is nothing more

[2] Chapter VI is the sequel of the preceding. There ought to have been some mention of *Shan* or "Spirit" in chapter 5. It is the first character in this chapter, and the two characters that follow show that it is here resumed for the purpose of being explained. As it does not occur in chapter 5, we must suppose that the author of it here brings forward and explains the idea of it that was in his mind. Many of the commentators recognize this.

Two other peculiarities in the style of the chapter are pointed out and explained (after a fashion) by Tshui Ching (earlier, probably, than the Sung Dynasty): "The action of six of the trigrams is described, but no mention is made of *Chien* or *Khwan.* But heaven and earth do nothing, and yet do everything; hence they are able to perfect the spirit-like subtilty of the action of thunder, wind, and the other things. Moreover, we have the trigram *Kan* mentioned, the only one mentioned by its name, instead of our reading 'mountains.' The reason is, that the putting in motion, the scattering, the parching, and the moistening, are all the palpable effects of thunder, wind, fire, and water. But what is ascribed to *Kan,* the ending and the recommencing all things, is not so evident of mountains. On this account the name of the trigram is given, while the things in nature represented by the trigrams are given in those other cases. The style suitable in each case is employed."

effective than wind; for drying them up there is nothing more parching than fire; for giving them pleasure and satisfaction there is nothing more grateful than a lake or marsh; for moistening them there is nothing more enriching than water; for bringing them to an end and making them begin again there is nothing more fully adapted than *Kan*. Thus water and fire contribute together to the one object; thunder and wind do not act contrary to each other; mountains and collections of water interchange their influences. It is in this way, that they are able to change and transform, and to give completion to all things.

Chapter VII. 11. *Chien* is the symbol of strength; *Khwan*, of docility; *Chan*, of stimulus to movement; *Sun*, of penetration; *Khan*, of what is precipitous and perilous; *Li*, of what is bright and what is catching; *Kan*, of stoppage or arrest; and *Tui*, of pleasure and satisfaction.

Chapter VIII. 12.[3] *Chien* suggests the idea of a horse; *Khwan*, that of an ox; *Chan*, that of the dragon; *Sun*, that of a fowl; *Khan*, that of a pig; *Li*, that of a pheasant; *Kan*, that of a dog; and *Tui*, that of a sheep.

Chapter IX. 13.[4] *Chien* suggests the idea of the head; *Khwan*, that of the belly; *Chan*, that of the feet; *Sun*, that of the thighs; *Khan*, that of the ears; *Li*, that of the eyes; *Kan*, that of the hands, and *Tui*, that of the mouth.

Chapter X. 14. *Chien* is the symbol of heaven, and hence has the appellation of father. *Khwan* is the symbol of earth, and hence has the appellation of mother. *Chan* shows a first application of *Khwan* to *Chien*, resulting in getting the first of its male or undivided lines, and hence is called " the oldest son." *Sun* shows a first application of *Chien* to *Khwan*, resulting in getting the first of its female or divided lines,

[3] Chapter VIII. In the Great Appendix, it is said that Fu-hsi, in making his trigrams, was guided by " the consideration of things apart from his own person." Of such things we have a specimen here. The creatures are assigned, in their classes, to the different trigrams, symbolizing the ideas in the last chapter. We must not make any difference of sex in translating their names.

[4] Chapter IX. Fu-hsi found also " things near at hand, in his own person," while making the trigrams. We have here a specimen of such things.

and hence is called "the oldest daughter." *Khan* shows a second application of *Khwan* to *Chien*, resulting in getting the second of its male or undivided lines, and hence is called "the second son." *Li* shows a second application of *Chien* to *Khwan*, resulting in getting the second of its female or divided lines, and hence is called "the second daughter." *Kan* shows a third application of *Khwan* to *Chien*, resulting in getting the third of its male or undivided lines, and hence is called "the youngest son." *Tui* shows a third application of *Chien* to *Khwan*, resulting in getting the third of its female or divided lines, and hence is called "the youngest daughter."

Chapter XI. 15. *Chien* suggests the idea of heaven; of a circle; of a ruler; of a father; of jade; of metal; of cold; of ice; of deep red; of a good horse; of an old horse; of a thin horse; of a piebald horse; and of the fruit of trees.

16. *Khwan* suggests the idea of the earth; of a mother; of cloth; of a caldron; of parsimony; of a turning lathe; of a young heifer; of a large wagon; of what is variegated; of a multitude; and of a handle and support. Among soils it denotes what is black.

17. *Chan* suggests the idea of thunder; of the dragon; of the union of the azure and the yellow; of development; of a great highway; of the eldest son; of decision and vehemence; of bright young bamboos; of sedges and rushes; among horses, of the good neigher; of one whose white hind-leg appears, of the prancer, and of one with a white star in his forehead. Among the productions of husbandry it suggests the idea of what returns to life from its disappearance beneath the surface, of what in the end becomes the strongest, and of what is most luxuriant.

18. *Sun* suggests the idea of wood; of wind; of the oldest daughter; of a plumb-line; of a carpenter's square; of being white; of being long; of being lofty; of advancing and receding; of want of decision; and of strong scents. It suggests in the human body the idea of deficiency of hair; of a wide forehead; of a large development of the white of the eye. Among tendencies, it suggests the close pursuit of gain, even to making three hundred per cent. in the market.

19. *Khan* suggests the idea of water; of channels and ditches for draining and irrigation; of being hidden and lying concealed; of being now straight and now crooked; of a bow, and of a wheel. As referred to man, it suggests the idea of an increase of anxiety; of distress of mind; of pain in the ears; it is the trigram of the blood; it suggests the idea of what is red. As referred to horses, it suggests the idea of the horse with an elegant spine; of one with a high spirit; of one with a drooping head; of one with a thin hoof; and of one with a shambling step. As referred to carriages, it suggests one that encounters many risks. It suggests what goes right through; the moon; a thief. Referred to trees, it suggests that which is strong and firm-hearted.

20. *Li* suggests the emblem of fire; of the sun; of lightning; of the second daughter; of buff-coat and helmet; of spear and sword. Referred to men, it suggests the large belly. It is the trigram of a dryness. It suggests the emblem of a turtle; of a crab; of a spiral univalve; of the mussel; and of the tortoise. Referred to trees, it suggests one which is hollow and rotten above.

21. *Kan* suggests the emblem of a mountain; of a by-path; of a small rock; of a gateway; of the fruits of trees and creeping plants; of a porter or a eunuch; of the ring finger; of the dog; of the rat; of birds with powerful bills; among trees, of those which are strong, with many joints.

22. *Tui* suggests the emblem of a low-lying collection of water; of the youngest daughter; of a sorceress; of the mouth and tongue; of the decay and putting down of things in harvest; of the removal of fruits hanging from the stems or branches; among soils, of what is strong and salt; of a concubine; and of a sheep.[5]

[5] Chapter XI may be made to comprehend all the paragraphs from the 15th to the end, and shows how universally the ideas underlying the Yi are diffused through the world of nature. The quality of the several trigrams will be found with more or less of truth, and with less or more of fancy, in the objects mentioned in connection with them.

END OF APPENDIX FIVE OF THE YI KING

This is the end of this publication.

Any remaining blank pages are for our book binding requirements and are blank on purpose.

To search thousands of interesting publications like this one, please remember to visit our website at:

http://www.kessinger.net

CPSIA information can be obtained at www.ICGtesting.com
Printed in the USA
BVOW02s1023101114

374431BV00024B/1042/P